EQUALITY
& JUSTICE

In the Words of 'Abdu'l-Bahá

BAHÁ'Í
PUBLISHING

WILMETTE, ILLINOIS

Bahá'í Publishing
401 Greenleaf Avenue, Wilmette, Illinois 60091
Copyright © 2021 by the National Spiritual Assembly
of the Bahá'ís of the United States
All rights reserved. Published 2021

Printed in the United States of America on acid-free paper ∞
24 23 22 21   4 3 2 1

ISBN 978-1-61851-198-0

Cover design by Carlos Esparza
Book design by Patrick Falso

Extract 28 is from *Bahá'í Prayers*. Wilmette, IL: Bahá'í Publishing Trust, 2002.

Extract 19 is from *The Secret of Divine Civilization*. Wilmette, IL: Bahá'í Publishing, 2007.

Extracts 5, 25 are from *Selections from the Writings of 'Abdu'l-Bahá*. Wilmette, IL: Bahá'í Publishing, 2010.

Extract 14 is from *'Abdu'l-Bahá in London: Addresses and Notes of Conversations*. London: Bahá'í Publishing Trust, 1982.

Extracts 1, 4, 10, 20, 22, 23, 27 are from *Paris Talks: Addresses Given by 'Abdu'l-Bahá in Paris in 1911*. Wilmette, IL: Bahá'í Publishing, 2011.

Extracts 2, 3, 6–9, 11–13, 15–18, 21, 24, 26 are from *The Promulgation of Universal Peace: Talks Delivered by 'Abdu'l-Bahá during His Visit to the United States and Canada in 1912*. Wilmette, IL: Bahá'í Publishing, 2012.

'Abdu'l-Bahá

November 2021 will mark the hundredth anniversary of the passing of a figure beloved by many. 'Abdu'l-Bahá, meaning *Servant of the Glory,* is the title assumed by Abbás Effendi (1844–1921), the son and appointed successor of Bahá'u'lláh—the Prophet and Founder of the Bahá'í Faith. 'Abdu'l-Bahá shared a lifetime of exile with his Father at the hands of the Persian and Ottoman Empires, and was a prisoner for forty years. Despite the severe hardships that characterized his life, he dedicated his energy to the service of others and radiated joy and selfless contentment at all times. His charitable deeds and undiscriminating love for all are well documented in the accounts of countless souls who crossed his path, and his timeless and deep wisdom is recorded extensively in both his written works and in the transcripts of his many public addresses. He is known by Bahá'ís as the perfect exemplar of the Faith's teachings.

1

Every human being has the right to live; they have a right to rest, and to a certain amount of well-being. As a rich man is able to live in his palace surrounded by luxury and the greatest comfort, so should a poor man be able to have the necessaries of life. Nobody should die of hunger; everybody should have sufficient clothing; one man should not live in excess while another has no possible means of existence.

Let us try with all the strength we have to bring about happier conditions, so that no single soul may be destitute.

2

The first teaching is that man should investigate reality, for reality is contrary to dogmatic interpretations and imitations of ancestral forms of belief to which all nations and peoples adhere so tenaciously. These blind imitations are contrary to the fundamental basis of the divine religions, for the divine religions in their central and essential teaching are based upon unity, love and peace, whereas these variations and imitations have ever been productive of warfare, sedition and strife. Therefore, all souls should consider it incumbent upon them to investigate reality. Reality is one; and when found, it will unify all mankind. Reality is the love of God. Reality is the knowledge of God. Reality is justice. Reality is the oneness or solidarity of mankind. Reality is international peace. Reality is the knowledge of verities. Reality unifies humanity.

3

Bahá'u'lláh also taught that prejudices—whether religious, racial, patriotic or political—are destructive to the foundations of human development. Prejudices of any kind are the destroyers of human happiness and welfare. Until they are dispelled, the advancement of the world of humanity is not possible; yet racial, religious and national biases are observed everywhere. For thousands of years the world of humanity has been agitated and disturbed by prejudices. As long as it prevails, warfare, animosity and hatred will continue. Therefore, if we seek to establish peace, we must cast aside this obstacle; for otherwise, agreement and composure are not to be attained.

4

Oh, friends of God, be living examples of justice! So that by the Mercy of God, the world may see in your actions that you manifest the attributes of justice and mercy.

5

Ye observe how the world is divided against itself, how many a land is red with blood and its very dust is caked with human gore. . . . From every aspect, humankind hath sunken low. Loud are the piercing cries of fatherless children; loud the mothers' anguished voices, reaching to the skies.

And the breeding ground of all these tragedies is prejudice: prejudice of race and nation, of religion, of political opinion; and the root cause of prejudice is blind imitation of the past—imitation in religion, in racial attitudes, in national bias, in politics. So long as this aping of the past persisteth, just so long will the foundations of the social order be blown to the four winds, just so long will humanity be continually exposed to direst peril.

6

Bahá'u'lláh has proclaimed the oneness of the world of humanity. He has caused various nations and divergent creeds to unite. He has declared that difference of race and color is like the variegated beauty of flowers in a garden. If you enter a garden, you will see yellow, white, blue, red flowers in profusion and beauty—each radiant within itself and although different from the others, lending its own charm to them. Racial difference in the human kingdom is similar. If all the flowers in a garden were of the same color, the effect would be monotonous and wearying to the eye.

Therefore, Bahá'u'lláh hath said that the various races of humankind lend a composite harmony and beauty of color to the whole. Let all associate, therefore, in this great human garden even as flowers grow and blend together side by side without discord or disagreement between them.

7

. . . the oneness of humanity shall be recognized and established. All men are the servants of God. He has created all; He is the Provider and Preserver; He is loving to all. Inasmuch as He is just and kind, why should we be unjust toward each other?

8

. . . there must be an equality of rights between men and women. Women shall receive an equal privilege of education. This will enable them to qualify and progress in all degrees of occupation and accomplishment. For the world of humanity possesses two wings: man and woman. If one wing remains incapable and defective, it will restrict the power of the other, and full flight will be impossible. Therefore, the completeness and perfection of the human world are dependent upon the equal development of these two wings.

9

. . . become leaders in the effort to establish the oneness of humankind. What is higher than this responsibility? In the Kingdom of God no service is greater, and in the estimation of the Prophets, including Jesus Christ, there is no deed so estimable.

10

Justice is not limited, it is a universal quality. Its operation must be carried out in all classes, from the highest to the lowest. Justice must be sacred, and the rights of all the people must be considered. Desire for others only that which you desire for yourselves. Then shall we rejoice in the Sun of Justice, which shines from the Horizon of God.

11

God is not partial and is no respecter of persons. He has made provision for all. The harvest comes forth for everyone. The rain showers upon everybody and the heat of the sun is destined to warm everyone. The verdure of the earth is for everyone. Therefore, there should be for all humanity the utmost happiness, the utmost comfort, the utmost well-being.

But if conditions are such that some are happy and comfortable and some in misery, some are accumulating exorbitant wealth and others are in dire want—under such a system it is impossible for man to be happy and impossible for him to win the good pleasure of God. God is kind to all. The good pleasure of God consists in the welfare of all the individual members of mankind.

12

To accept and observe a distinction which God has not intended in creation is ignorance and superstition. The fact which is to be considered, however, is that woman, having formerly been deprived, must now be allowed equal opportunities with man for education and training. There must be no difference in their education. Until the reality of equality between man and woman is fully established and attained, the highest social development of mankind is not possible.

13

All the heavenly Books are the written word of love. If they prove to be the cause of prejudice and human estrangement, they have become fruitless. Therefore, religious prejudice is especially opposed to the will and command of God. Racial and national prejudices which separate mankind into groups and branches, likewise, have a false and unjustifiable foundation, for all men are the children of Adam and essentially of one family.

14

The gift of God to this enlightened age is the knowledge of the oneness of mankind and of the fundamental oneness of religion.

15

You must manifest complete love and affection toward all mankind. Do not exalt yourselves above others, but consider all as your equals, recognizing them as the servants of one God. Know that God is compassionate toward all; therefore, love all from the depths of your hearts, prefer all religionists before yourselves, be filled with love for every race, and be kind toward the people of all nationalities.

16

According to the teachings of Bahá'u'lláh all religious, racial, patriotic and political prejudice must be abandoned, for these are the destroyers of the real foundation of humanity.

17

Consider the prejudice of patriotism. This is one globe, one land, one country. God did not divide it into national boundaries. He created all the continents without national divisions. Why should we make such division ourselves? These are but imaginary lines and boundaries.

18

Prejudices of all kinds—whether religious, racial, patriotic or political—are destructive of divine foundations in man. All the warfare and bloodshed in human history have been the outcome of prejudice. This earth is one home and native land. God has created mankind with equal endowment and right to live upon the earth. As a city is the home of all its inhabitants although each may have his individual place of residence therein, so the earth's surface is one wide native land or home for all races of humankind. Racial prejudice or separation into nations . . . is unnatural and proceeds from human motive and ignorance. All are the children and servants of God. Why should we be separated by artificial and imaginary boundaries?

19

. . . if a judicious and resourceful individual should initiate measures which would universally enrich the masses of the people, there could be no undertaking greater than this, and it would rank in the sight of God as the supreme achievement, for such a benefactor would supply the needs and insure the comfort and well-being of a great multitude. Wealth is most commendable, provided the entire population is wealthy. If, however, a few have inordinate riches while the rest are impoverished, and no fruit or benefit accrues from that wealth, then it is only a liability to its possessor. If, on the other hand, it is expended for the promotion of knowledge, the founding of elementary and other schools, the encouragement of art and industry, the training of orphans and the poor—in brief, if it is dedicated to the welfare of society—its possessor will stand out before God and man as the most excellent of all who live on earth and will be accounted as one of the people of paradise.

20

Concerning the prejudice of race: it is an illusion, a superstition pure and simple! For God created us all of one race. There were no differences in the beginning, for we are all descendants of Adam. In the beginning, also, there were no limits and boundaries between the different lands; no part of the earth belonged more to one people than to another. In the sight of God there is no difference between the various races. Why should man invent such a prejudice? How can we uphold war caused by an illusion?

21

The earth is one native land, one home; and all mankind are the children of one Father. God has created them, and they are the recipients of His compassion. Therefore, if anyone offends another, he offends God. It is the wish of our heavenly Father that every heart should rejoice and be filled with happiness, that we should live together in felicity and joy. The obstacle to human happiness is racial or religious prejudice, the competitive struggle for existence and inhumanity toward each other.

22

I hope that each one of you will become just, and direct your thoughts towards the unity of mankind; that you will never harm your neighbors nor speak ill of anyone; that you will respect the rights of all men, and be more concerned for the interests of others than for your own. Thus will you become torches of Divine justice, acting in accordance with the Teaching of Bahá'u'lláh, who, during His life, bore innumerable trials and persecutions in order to show forth to the world of mankind the virtues of the World of Divinity, making it possible for you to realize the supremacy of the spirit, and to rejoice in the Justice of God.

23

Women have equal rights with men upon earth; in religion and society they are a very important element. As long as women are prevented from attaining their highest possibilities, so long will men be unable to achieve the greatness which might be theirs.

24

We must set aside bias and prejudice. We must abandon the imitations of ancestors and forefathers. We ourselves must investigate reality and be fair in judgment.

25

For every era hath a spirit; the spirit of this illumined era lieth in the teachings of Bahá'u'lláh. For these lay the foundation of the oneness of the world of humanity and promulgate universal brotherhood. They are founded upon the unity of science and religion and upon investigation of truth. They uphold the principle that religion must be the cause of amity, union and harmony among men. They establish the equality of both sexes and propound economic principles which are for the happiness of individuals. They diffuse universal education, that every soul may as much as possible have a share of knowledge. They abrogate and nullify religious, racial, political, patriotic and economic prejudices and the like. Those teachings . . . are the cause of the illumination and the life of the world of humanity. Whoever promulgateth them will verily be assisted by the Kingdom of God.

26

. . . sources of human dissension are political, racial and patriotic prejudices. These have been removed by Bahá'u'lláh. He has said, and has guarded His statement by rational proofs from the Holy Books, that the world of humanity is one race, the surface of the earth one place of residence and that these imaginary racial barriers and political boundaries are without right or foundation.

27

Bahá'u'lláh has rent the veil of prejudice and superstition which was stifling the souls of men. Let us pray to God that the breath of the Holy Spirit may again give hope and refreshment to the people, awakening in them a desire to do the Will of God.

28

O Thou kind Lord! Unite all. Let the religions agree and make the nations one, so that they may see each other as one family and the whole earth as one home. May they all live together in perfect harmony.